D1505948

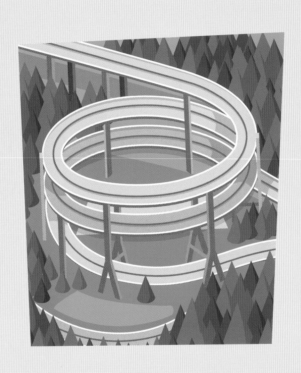

*Author:*

**Ian Graham** earned a degree in applied physics at City University, London. He then earned a degree in journalism. Since becoming a freelance author and journalist, he has written more than 250 children's nonfiction books.

*Series creator:*

**David Salariya** was born in Dundee, Scotland. He has illustrated a wide range of books and has created and designed many new series for publishers in the UK and overseas. David established The Salariya Book Company in 1989. He lives in Brighton, England, with his wife, illustrator Shirley Willis, and their son, Jonathan.

*Artists:*

Diego Vaisberg, Bryan Beach, Zern Liew, Anton V. Tokarev, Dilk Feros, and Shutterstock.

*Editor:*

Nick Pierce

Published in Great Britain in 2019 by
**The Salariya Book Company Ltd**
25 Marlborough Place, Brighton BN1 1UB

Library of Congress Cataloging-in-Publication Data

Names: Graham, Ian, 1953- author. | Vaisberg, Diego, illustrator. | Beach, Bryan, illustrator.
Title: The science of bridges and tunnels : the art of engineering / written by Ian Graham ; artists, Diego Vaisberg, Bryan Beach.
Description: New York, NY : Franklin Watts, an imprint of Scholastic Inc., 2019. | Series: Science of... | Includes index.
Identifiers: LCCN 2018031804| ISBN 9780531131992 (library binding) | ISBN 9780531133996 (pbk.)
Subjects: LCSH: Civil engineering--Juvenile literature. | Bridges--Design and construction--Juvenile literature. | Tunnels--Design and construction--Juvenile literature.
Classification: LCC TA149 .G69 2019 | DDC 624--dc23

Published in 2019 in the United States
by Franklin Watts
An imprint of Scholastic Inc.

Printed and bound in China.
Printed on paper from sustainable sources.
1 2 3 4 5 6 7 8 9 10 R 28 27 26 25 24 23 22 21 20 19

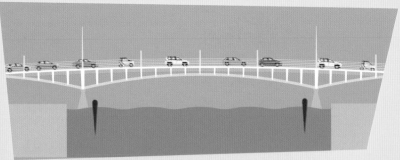

# The Science of Bridges and Tunnels

## The Art of Engineering

written by
Ian Graham

Franklin Watts®
An Imprint of Scholastic Inc.

# Contents

# Introduction

People have needed to cross rivers and valleys for as long as there have been people on Earth. At first, they made simple bridges from whatever natural materials they could find, mainly slabs of stone, tree trunks, and woven plant fibers. Tunneling is as ancient as bridge building. The first tunnels were dug for mining useful materials like flint and moving water. Later, bigger tunnels were built for transportation. The first bridge and tunnel builders learned what worked and what didn't by trial and error. Then scientists and engineers discovered the laws of nature that apply to bridges and tunnels, and they understood the strengths and weaknesses of materials better, too. New materials, such as concrete and steel, made it possible to build new types of bridges and longer, deeper tunnels. Today, the design of a new bridge or tunnel is a mixture of art and engineering.

5

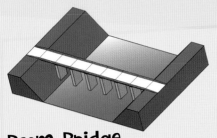

## Beam Bridge

A beam bridge is supported at each end. Any weight on the bridge presses down on the beam. The top is compressed and the bottom is stretched (in tension).

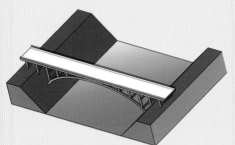

## Arch Bridge

An arch bridge works based on compression. Arch bridges made of stone or brick resist compression forces, making the bridge strong.

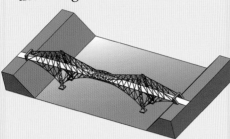

## Cantilever Bridge

A cantilever is a beam held at only one end. A weight pressing down on a cantilever stretches the top and compresses the bottom.

# Types of Bridges

There are four basic types of bridges: beam, arch, cantilever, and suspension bridges. Four main types of forces act on all bridges. They are compression, tension, torsion, and shear. Compression is a pressing or squeezing force, tension is a pulling force, and torsion is a twisting force. Shear is the result of two forces acting in opposite directions, making parts slide past each other like scissor blades. Compression and tension are the most important. Bridge designers have to think about how these forces act on a bridge and design the bridge to resist them.

The oldest bridge still in use is a 2,900-year-old stone arch bridge over the river Meles in Izmir, Turkey. The remains of 3,600-year-old bridges have been found in Greece.

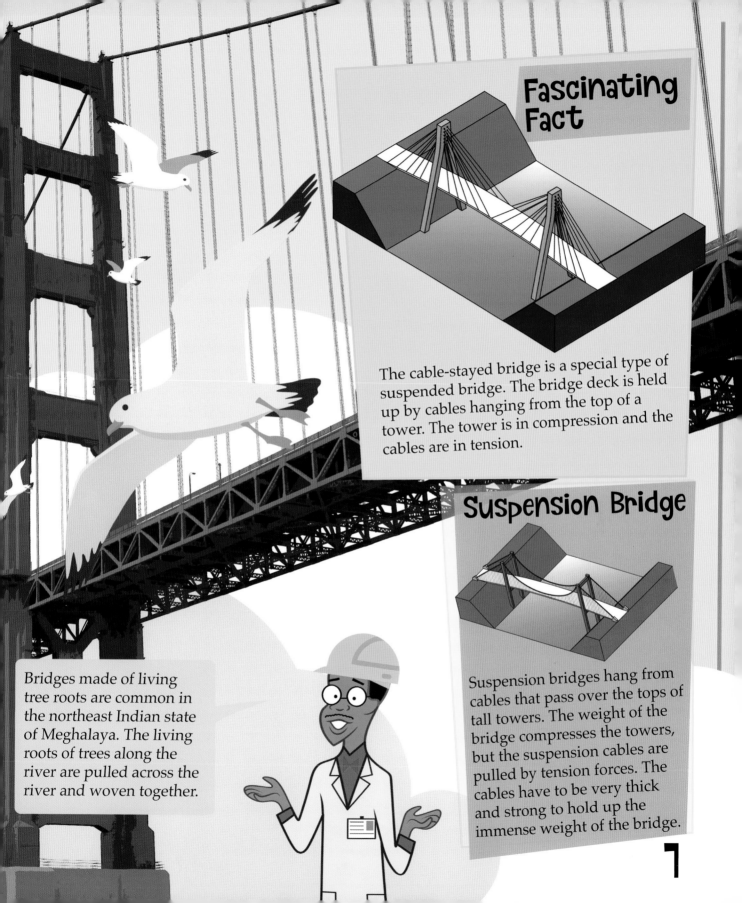

The cable-stayed bridge is a special type of suspended bridge. The bridge deck is held up by cables hanging from the top of a tower. The tower is in compression and the cables are in tension.

## Suspension Bridge

Suspension bridges hang from cables that pass over the tops of tall towers. The weight of the bridge compresses the towers, but the suspension cables are pulled by tension forces. The cables have to be very thick and strong to hold up the immense weight of the bridge.

Bridges made of living tree roots are common in the northeast Indian state of Meghalaya. The living roots of trees along the river are pulled across the river and woven together.

# Beam Bridges

eam bridges are simple and easy to build, but they can't span long gaps. They are rarely longer than about 250 feet (80 meters). They can be made longer by adding one beam bridge after another end to end. For thousands of years, the beams were made of solid stone or wood, but some modern beam bridges use steel boxes or frames instead of solid beams. The Lake Pontchartrain Causeway in Louisiana is two beam bridges beside each other. One, built in 1956, has 2,243 spans and the other, built in 1969, has 1,500 longer spans. Together, they form a bridge with a total length of 23.9 miles (38.5 kilometers).

## Can You Believe It?

The weight that a bridge has to support is divided into two parts—the live load and the dead load. The dead load is the weight of the bridge itself. The live load is the weight of traffic on the bridge.

The supports underneath a bridge are called piers, and the supports at the ends of a bridge are called abutments.

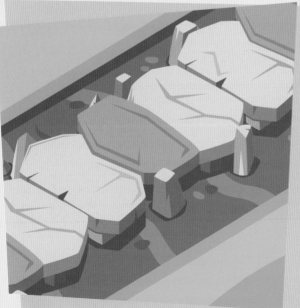

## Clapper Bridges

Ancient beam bridges made of slabs of stone are sometimes called clapper bridges. They were built from prehistoric times up to about the fifteenth century. They are low, flat bridges with lots of supports to hold them up.

It's so long I can't see the end!

## Truss Bridge

A truss bridge has a strong frame, called a truss, instead of a solid beam. A truss is very strong and is made of less material than a beam, so it's lighter than a solid beam bridge. Truss bridges became very popular in the nineteenth century.

A continuous span is one long bridge made up of a series of beam bridges joined together end to end.

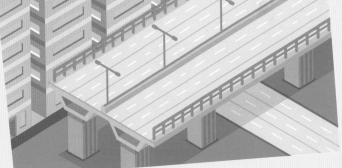

## Box Girder Beam Bridge

A box girder beam bridge has a hollow, box-shaped beam instead of a solid beam. It's made of concrete or steel. Box girders are also used to build various other types of bridges. Modern suspension bridges have a slender, hollow, box girder deck.

9

# Roman Arches

The Pont du Gard was built in France nearly 2,000 years ago to carry water across a valley. A bridge that carries water is called an aqueduct. Three rows of arches, one on top of another, carry the weight of the structure.

The weight of an arch tries to push the ends of the arch apart, so the ends have to be held firmly in place or the arch may collapse.

# Arch Bridges

The arch has been used for thousands of years. The ancient Romans were masters of building with arches. They used arches to support the weight of walls above doorways and windows in grand buildings, and they used arches to build bridges. The arch bridge is still one of the most popular types of bridges built today. One famous arch bridge is the Sydney Harbour Bridge in Australia. The arch is usually below the deck, supporting it from underneath, but the Sydney Harbour Bridge's deck runs through the arch. Because of its shape, this bridge is known as The Coat Hanger.

# Concrete Arches

Modern, high-quality concrete enables designers and engineers to produce beautiful, slender bridges that could not be built before. The Rich Street Bridge across the Scioto River in Columbus, Ohio, is supported by four lines of thin arches cast from high-strength, lightweight concrete.

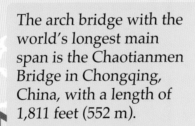

The arch bridge with the world's longest main span is the Chaotianmen Bridge in Chongqing, China, with a length of 1,811 feet (552 m).

# Fascinating Fact

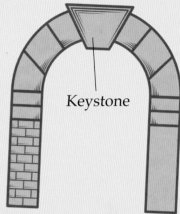

Keystone

While a stone arch is being built, it has no strength and can't stand up. It has to be supported and only becomes strong enough to stand by itself and bear weight when the final stone, called the keystone, is put in place to lock it together.

# Modern Arches

The Crown Prince Bridge in Germany is a modern take on the traditional arch bridge. The bridge deck is supported by shallow steel arches held out on each side of the bridge.

11

# Cantilever Bridges

The cantilever bridge was invented in the nineteenth century when new railways were being built and lots of new bridges were needed. Compared to beam bridges and arch bridges, cantilever bridges need fewer supports, so they were good for crossing busy rivers. A long cantilever bridge usually has a pair of cantilevers with a beam bridge between them, linking the cantilevers.

Ta-da!

The Quebec Bridge has the longest cantilever span in the world, at 1,801 feet (549 m), even though the bridge was built as long ago as 1919.

## Why It Works

In 1887, three of the engineers who designed the Forth Rail Bridge showed why it works. The man in the middle sits on the beam bridge linking two cantilevers. The other men each represent two cantilevers back-to-back. Their arms are in tension and the sticks below their arms are in compression.

Caisson workers can suffer from an illness that usually affects divers. If workers leave the high-pressure air in a caisson too quickly, bubbles can form in their blood. It's called decompression sickness.

I don't feel very well...

One of the first steel cantilever bridges, the Forth Rail Bridge (above), was built across the Firth of Forth in Scotland in the 1880s.

## A Solid Base

A giant chamber called a caisson, open at the bottom, is placed on the riverbed or seabed. High-pressure air inside keeps water out. Workers dig out the mud inside and the caisson sinks until it rests on rock. Then it is filled with concrete to form a solid support for a bridge.

13

# Suspension Bridges

## Massive Anchors

The weight of a suspension bridge tries to pull the ends of its suspension cables out of the ground, so they have to be locked in place by massive blocks of rock or concrete called anchorages. In Japan, each of the Akashi Kaikyo Bridge's anchorages weighs 390,000 tons.

The biggest bridges are so long that they are affected by the curved shape of Earth's surface. The tops of their towers are farther apart than their bases.

Suspension bridges became popular in the twentieth century because they could span longer distances than cantilever bridges without lots of supports, or piers, underneath. They were ideal for spanning wide rivers and bays where it would be difficult to build a line of piers. The bridge is held up from above by vertical cables called hangers, or suspenders. The suspenders hang from the bridge's main suspension cables, which are anchored at each end of the bridge. One of the most famous suspension bridges is the Golden Gate Bridge across the entrance to San Francisco Bay in California.

## Spinning Wire

Suspension cables are made of thousands of thin wires bundled together. The Golden Gate Bridge's suspension cables are about 3.3 feet (1 m) thick. Each cable is made of 27,572 pencil-thin wires. Stringing the wires from one end of the bridge to the other is a process called cable spinning.

*Cross-section of cable wire*

*Wires bundled together into cable*

## Simple Bridges

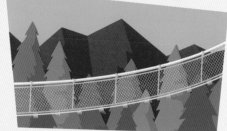

Some suspension bridges are still made in the same way as ancient rope bridges, but using modern materials. The Capilano Suspension Bridge in Canada is a steel cable suspension footbridge. Walkers use it to cross the Capilano River through the treetops in a tourist park in Vancouver.

The first modern suspension bridge is the Menai Bridge between Wales and the island of Anglesey in England. It opened in 1826 and is still in use today.

## Can You Believe It?

The Akashi Kaikyo Bridge in Japan is 3.3 feet (1 m) longer than planned. While it was being built, an earthquake moved its towers farther apart. The deck was made a little longer to fill the gap.

# Building Bridges to Last

One of the strangest materials used to build bridges is plastic water bottles. In 2014, a bridge made of 104,500 bottles was built across the Bega River in Romania.

## Tough Stuff

Reinforced concrete is often used to build bridges. It's made of concrete with steel rods called rebars embedded in it. Concrete is good at resisting compression, and steel is good at resisting tension (stretching). Together, they make a very strong building material.

ngineers build bridges to last by designing them to withstand the forces that try to destroy them. The different parts of a bridge are built from different materials. The materials are carefully chosen to resist the compression or tension forces acting on each part. One of the oldest bridges in the world that is still in use today is China's Anji Bridge, also known as the Zhaozhou Bridge. It is a stone arch bridge that was completed in the year 605 CE. It has survived ten floods, eight wars, and numerous earthquakes.

# Strong Shapes

The steel plates and girders that make up parts of bridges are often linked together in a way that makes triangles, because a triangle is a very strong shape. Steel girders linked together in triangles combine strength and light weight, and let the wind blow through the structure.

This bridge must be strong—it's got lots of triangles!

A triangle is strong because each of its sides locks the other two sides into position.

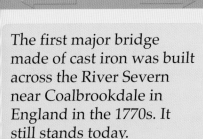

The first major bridge made of cast iron was built across the River Severn near Coalbrookdale in England in the 1770s. It still stands today.

# Can You Believe It?

The secret ingredient that made Roman concrete so tough and long-lasting was volcanic ash. The ash was called pozzolana. It helped bind the concrete together very strongly, and it resisted damage from seawater.

Maybe we should leave before the volcano erupts?

# Hinges

Iron and steel expand when they warm up and shrink again when they cool down. The top of the Sydney Harbour Bridge can rise or fall by up to 7 inches (18 centimeters) because of temperature changes. Giant hinges at the ends of the arches let the bridge do this without breaking up.

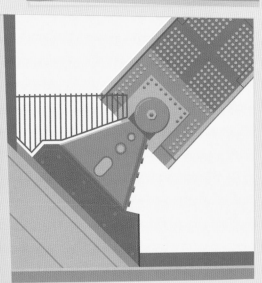

## Spiral Bridges

The Kawazu-Nanadaru Loop Bridge in Japan is a spiral bridge. It connects the road on one mountainside with another road on the next mountainside 148 feet (45 m) below.

# Bridging Heights

**B**ridges usually link two riverbanks or two sides of a valley at the same level, but some bridges link two points at very different heights. Some of them do it with a roadway that spirals in tight circles, like a spiral staircase. These spiral roads are also used in places where there isn't room on the ground for the long approach roads that lead up to a bridge. Cars can also be lifted by an elevator that brings them up to a higher level.

The Falkirk Wheel is so well-balanced that lifting boats from one canal to another uses the same amount of energy as boiling eight pots of water.

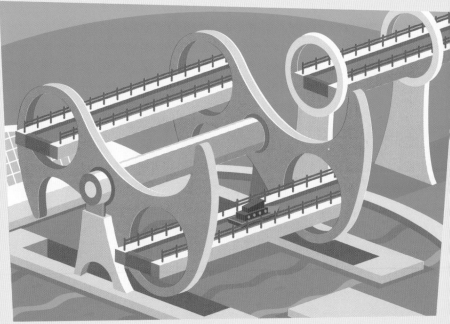

The Falkirk Wheel in Scotland bridges the gap between one waterway and another 79 feet (24 m) below it. Each end of the wheel can hold four 66-foot-long (20 m) barges in a tank of 66,000 gallons (250,000 liters) of water.

# Transporter Bridge

A transporter bridge moves a section of roadway carrying a number of vehicles from one side of a river to the other.

The piece of road with safety fences all around, called a gondola, is slung underneath a bridge span.

It's a long way down!

The transporter bridge was invented in 1872 and the first one was built in Spain in 1893. Once popular, fewer than a dozen transporter bridges are left worldwide.

## Fascinating Fact

Vertical-lift bridges let boats pass by moving the whole bridge straight upward to leave a clear water channel underneath. Submersible bridges move in the opposite direction. They sink straight down under the water.

# Strange Spans

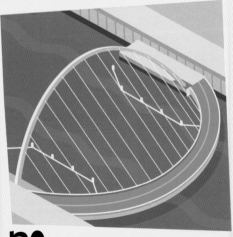

## Blinking Eye

The Gateshead Millennium Bridge in England is also known as the Blinking Eye Bridge. When it tilts to let river traffic pass underneath, it looks like an eye opening.

**D**esigners and engineers are always thinking of new ways to build bridges. They've built bridges that float and bridges that open by rolling up. The Netherlands has lots of bridges because it has so many rivers and canals crisscrossing roads. One of the strangest-looking is the Slauerhoffbrug (flying drawbridge) at a road crossing over the Harlinger Vaart River. A pair of arms next to the river lifts a square section of road to let boats pass. It's a type of bridge called a tail bridge.

# Roll Up, Roll Up!

Rolling Bridge, designed by Thomas Heatherwick, opens by curling upward like a mechanical worm and rolling up to form an octagon (eight-sided shape) on one side of the water. It is the only bridge of its type anywhere in the world.

## Low Profile

The Millennium Bridge across the River Thames in London is a suspension bridge with a difference. Its suspension cables lie alongside the bridge deck, not above it, to give clear views across the river! The stiffness and strength of the bridge comes from tension in the cables.

The Millennium Bridge in London wobbled unexpectedly and was closed for a year and a half while parts called dampers were installed to stop the unwanted motion.

## Can You Believe It?

Bridges are heavy structures weighing thousands of tons, but it is possible to make bridges that float. Ancient floating bridges rested on top of boats or barges. Modern floating bridges float on hollow concrete pontoons.

# When Bridges Go Wrong

## Sudden Collapse

On August 1, 2007, a steel arch bridge across the Mississippi River in Minneapolis, Minnesota, suddenly dropped into the river. Steel sheets called gusset plates, designed to strengthen the bridge, were too thin and weak. Eventually, one of them gave way and the whole bridge collapsed.

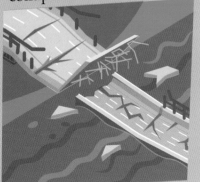

Bridges are designed to be safe and built to last for decades, but on rare occasions something goes wrong. A mistake might have been made in a bridge's design, or perhaps an error was made during construction. A vital part might break, or perhaps corrosion causes a weakness. Extreme weather can cause damage, too. On December 28, 1879, the iron bridge across the River Tay in Scotland collapsed as a passenger train crossed it. The bridge fell mainly because it wasn't strong enough to withstand the strong wind blowing on that night.

The weather at bridges is carefully monitored. If the wind is strong enough to blow vehicles over, or ice starts falling onto the roadway, the bridge is closed.

# Hurricane!

In 2005, Hurricane Katrina swept over New Orleans, Louisiana. A rising swell of water tore into the Interstate-10 bridge on Lake Pontchartrain. It pushed dozens of sections of the bridge off their piers. Some were shifted out of position. Others disappeared into the lake.

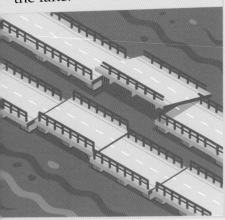

# Traffic Crash

Bridges are sometimes damaged by traffic accidents. In 2013, a truck crashed into part of the Interstate-5 Skagit River Bridge in Washington State, and weakened the bridge so much that part of it collapsed. The bridge was nearly 60 years old. More modern bridges are designed to survive accidents like this.

No one knows how many bridges there are in the whole world, but there are about 600,000 in the United States alone.

# Can You Believe It?

Two suspension bridges in Britain and France collapsed in the nineteenth century while soldiers were marching across them. As a result, soldiers were ordered to walk, not march, across bridges.

Left, right, left, right!

# Building Tunnels

The same four forces that act on bridges also act on tunnels—compression, tension, torsion, and shear. The ground that surrounds a tunnel presses inward and tries to crush it. The tunnel's shape and the materials used to construct it have to resist these powerful forces. There are three main ways to build a tunnel. It can be blasted with explosives, dug by hand, or bored through the ground by a huge, worm-like tunneling machine called a tunnel boring machine, or TBM.

## Grinding Teeth

The front of a TBM slowly rotates. Teeth or cutting wheels grind away the rock. The rock falls onto a conveyor belt, which carries it away to waiting rail wagons. Then jacks push the machine forward while it grinds away more rock, carving out a perfectly round tunnel.

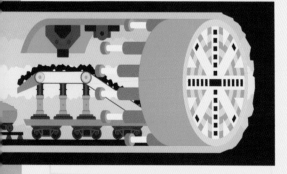

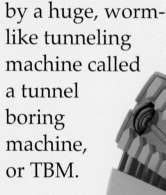

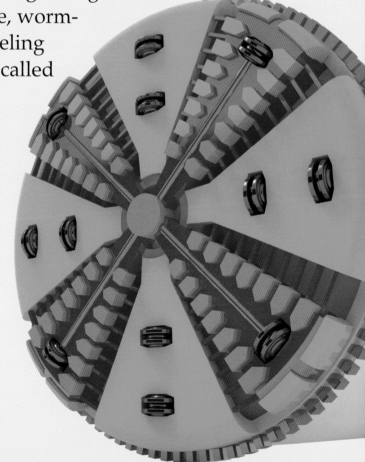

The world's first underground railway opened in London in 1863. Other cities quickly followed. The New York City Subway opened in 1904.

# Lining a Tunnel

Behind a TBM's rotating cutterhead, a crane lifts heavy concrete blocks into place to line the tunnel. A round tunnel lined with interlocking concrete blocks is strong enough to resist the crushing force of the ground. The force is spread evenly around the whole tunnel.

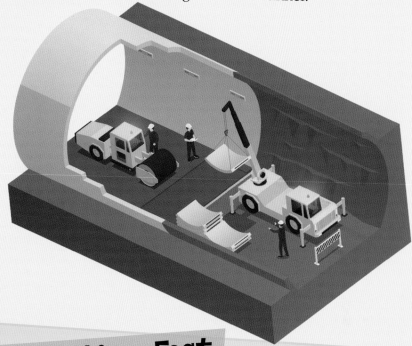

# Blasting

If rock is too hard for a TBM to cut through, it has to be blasted out. Holes drilled in the rock are packed with explosives. The explosions shatter the rock. Then the new tunnel face is blasted. This is repeated until the tunnel is completed.

3...2...1...

# Fascinating Fact

A tunneling method called tunnel jacking or box jacking involves using jacks to push a ready-made box-shaped concrete tunnel into position through soft ground. Then the earth is dug out of the tunnel.

# Tunneling Underwater

Tunneling underwater can be difficult and dangerous because the ground is often soft and there is a risk of water breaking through into the tunnel and flooding it. If a layer of the right type of rock is found, TBMs can be used to bore a tunnel through it. If not, a method called immersed tube might be used instead. The tunnel is laid on top of the riverbed or seabed.

The biggest undersea tunnel system is the Channel Tunnel between England and France. It is actually three tunnels—two rail tunnels and a service tunnel.

The Channel Tunnel was dug by eleven massive TBMs. Six dug the three tunnels under the sea, and the other five dug the inland parts of the tunnels.

## Holland Tunnel

The Holland Tunnel under the Hudson River in New York City was one of the first modern underwater road tunnels. It was the first tunnel to be fitted with fans to blow poisonous vehicle exhaust fumes out and bring fresh air in. It opened in 1927 and is still in use today.

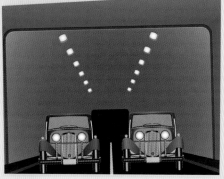

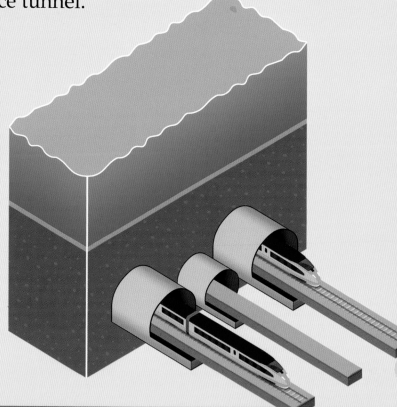

# Immersed Tube

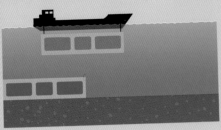
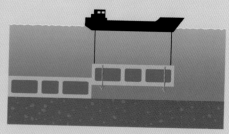

An immersed tube tunnel is built in sections and encased in concrete. Each section is sealed to keep water out. Then it's floated out to the right position and flooded to make it sink. The sections are joined together and the water is pumped out.

While digging a tunnel under the East River in New York in 1916, an accident caused three workers to shoot through the tunnel wall, riverbed, water, and into the air. One man survived!

## Long and Deep

The Seikan Tunnel between two Japanese islands is one of the longest and deepest undersea tunnels. It is 330 feet (100 m) below the seabed and 790 feet (240 m) below sea level. Almost half of the 33.5-mile (54 km) tunnel is under the sea.

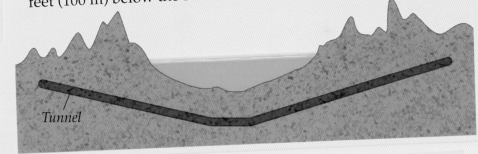

Tunnel

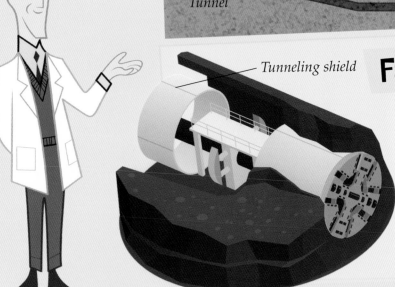

Tunneling shield

## Fascinating Fact

During tunneling, there is a risk of loose rock collapsing onto tunnelers. The front of a TBM is surrounded by a casing called a tunneling shield that stops the tunnel from collapsing until it can be lined.

The San Francisco-Oakland Bay Bridge is unique. It's a pair of bridges connected by a tunnel that goes through an island.

# Bridge-Tunnels

Transportation links sometimes need both a bridge and a tunnel. The distance to be spanned might be too long for a bridge alone, or the conditions might be too difficult for building a bridge the entire way. Tunnels are more expensive to construct than bridges, so in some places a bridge is built part of the way and a tunnel completes the link. If the bridge and tunnel meet in the middle of a waterway where there is no land, an island has to be built specially for the purpose.

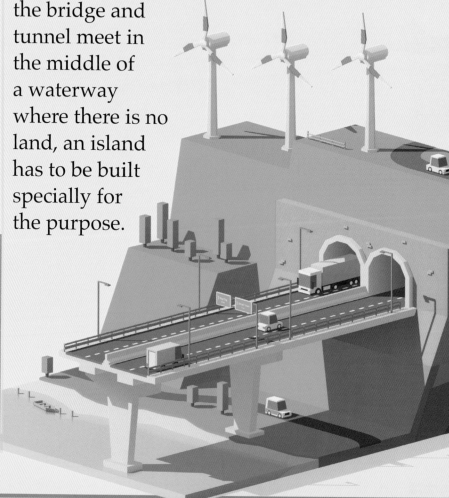

## Road to Nowhere

The Oresund Bridge from the Swedish coast appears to end on a tiny island in the middle of the Oresund Strait, but it actually connects with the Drogden Tunnel to Denmark. A completely high bridge would have interfered with airplanes in Copenhagen.

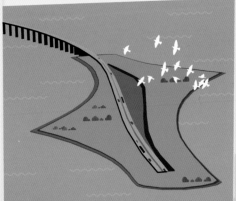

# Clear for Shipping

The Chesapeake Bay Bridge-Tunnel in Virginia has four bridges, two tunnels, and four artificial islands. The tunnels were built to cross two busy shipping lanes that are also important military seaways. The US Navy could not risk them being blocked by a collapsed bridge in wartime.

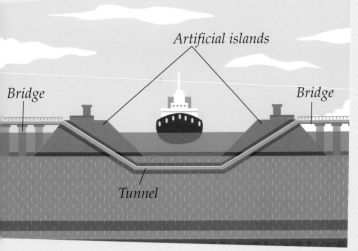

*Artificial islands*

*Bridge*  *Bridge*

*Tunnel*

## Sunken Tunnel

The Monitor-Merrimac Memorial Bridge-Tunnel is a four-lane road transport link between the cities of Newport News and Suffolk in Virginia. Completed in 1992, the 4,800-foot (1.5 km) tunnel section is an immersed tube. It was built in 15 sections on land and then sunk into position on the seabed.

The Oresund Bridge and tunnel were originally designed to connect with each other on an existing island called Saltholm, but they actually meet on an artificial (human-made) island, so that Saltholm's plants and animals remain protected.

## Fascinating Fact

Sailors on Tokyo Bay may notice something that looks like a sailboat, but it's the top of a ventilation shaft for the tunnel part of the Tokyo Bay Aqua Line.

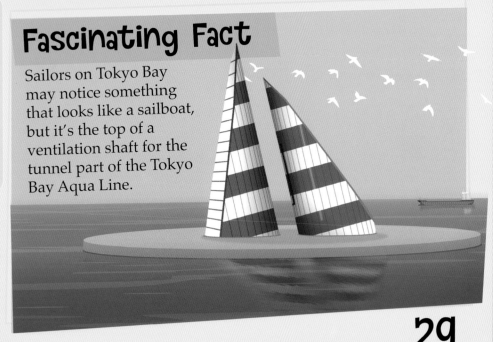

# Glossary

**Abutment** Blocks or structures at the ends of an arch, stopping the ends of the arch from pushing apart.

**Aqueduct** A bridge that carries water.

**Arch** A curved structure that holds up a roof, wall, or bridge.

**Barge** A long flat-bottomed cargo boat used on rivers and canals.

**Beam** A slab of stone, metal, or wood used to support a load.

**Box girder** A hollow beam.

**Caisson** A large chamber, open at the bottom, from which water is kept out by air pressure.

**Canal** An artificial waterway.

**Cantilever** A beam fixed or held at one end only.

**Causeway** A raised road or footpath across water or wet ground.

**Clapper bridge** A simple bridge made of slabs of stone laid on piles of rocks.

**Compression** A pressing or squeezing force.

**Concrete** A building material made from a mixture of sand, cement, stone (or gravel), and water.

**Corrosion** A chemical process that slowly changes and damages a material.

**Cutterhead** The rotating front of a tunnel boring machine with teeth or cutting wheels to cut through the rock in front of the machine.

**Dead load** The weight of a structure such as a bridge.

**Deck** The roadway of a bridge.

**Engineers** People who design, build, or repair engines, machines, or structures.

**Footbridge** A bridge designed to be walked across.

**Girder** A long iron or steel beam used to build structures such as bridges.

**Gusset plate** A sheet of metal fastened across a joint in a structure to strengthen it.

**Hanger** One of the vertical cables that hangs from a bridge's suspension cables and holds up the bridge deck.

**Hurricane** A violent, rotating tropical storm with strong winds and a clear area called an eye in the middle. Also known as a typhoon or cyclone in different parts of the world.

**Immersed tube** An underwater tunnel made of sections floated out, sunk into position, and linked together.

**Keystone** The stone at the center of an arch that locks the other parts of the arch together.

**Live load** The weight of people or vehicles on a bridge.

**Pier** One of the supports underneath a bridge that holds the bridge up.

**Pontoon** A boat or other floating structure that supports a floating bridge.

**Prehistoric** The time before written history.

**Rebar** Reinforcing bar; steel rod embedded in concrete to make reinforced concrete.

**Reinforced concrete** Concrete strengthened by having steel reinforcing bars (rebars) embedded in it.

**Roman concrete** A material used for construction work in Ancient Rome.

**Shear** The result of two forces acting in opposite directions, making parts slide past each other like scissor blades.

**Steel** A metal made of mainly iron and carbon.

# Index